This
NORMAL LIFE
belongs to:

- - - - - - - - - - - - -

C000069858

Steven Appleby's
NORMAL LIFE

BLOOMSBURY

MANY THANKS TO:
Liz Calder, Toby Swift, Nicola, Kasper de Graaf, Linda and Alan McCarthy, Frank and EVERYONE who went on the BBC Drama Blue Skies workshop and ALL at Bloomsbury for their unceasing support!

The BBC logo is a trademark of the British Broadcasting Corporation and is used under licence. BBC logo © BBC 1996

FIRST PUBLISHED 2001

Copyright Steven Appleby © 2001
The moral right of the author has been asserted

BLOOMSBURY Publishing Plc
38 Soho Square, London W1D 3HB

ISBN 0 7475 5614 8

Printed in Great Britain by Bath Press

INTRODUCTION

This autobiography is a sort-of companion to my BBC Radio 4 series, Steven Appleby's Normal Life, in which I reveal some of my more interestingly mundane memories.

Of course, most of you will have had similar experiences. Who hasn't gone to work, wondered about the meaning of life, been tempted by the Devil, abducted by aliens, and so on. These things are common to us all. It is their very normality which makes them relevant and therefore worthy of inclusion.

So, come on, don't be ashamed! You're normal. I'm normal. Let's stand up and be counted!

Welcome to my Normal Life...

POWER **YOUR** HOUSE WITH AN
ECOLOGICALLY FRIENDLY
HUMAN-SIZED **HAMSTER WHEEL!**

(CHILD OR ADULT SIZES!)

ONLY **8** HOURS PER DAY WILL RUN:
1 fridge
1 hot bath
1 TV and
1 video
INSTALL CHILD-SIZE TREADMILLS TO POWER THEIR COMPUTER GAMES!

IT'S GOOD EXERCISE and CHARACTER-BUILDING!

CONTENTS

HOW TO USE THIS BOOK

HOLD THE BOOK AT A COMFORTABLE DISTANCE IN FRONT OF YOUR EYES AND SCAN THE PAGES BY MOVING YOUR EYEBALLS FROM LEFT TO RIGHT AND SLOWLY FROM TOP TO BOTTOM. WHEN YOUR EYEBALLS REACH THE BOTTOM OF A RIGHT-HAND PAGE, USE ONE OF YOUR HANDS TO TURN OVER TO A FRESH PAGE. WHEN YOU HAVE PERUSED THE WHOLE BOOK, CLOSE IT AND PASS IT ON TO A FRIEND. OR BETTER STILL, PLACE THE BOOK BACK ON YOUR BOOKSHELF AND RECOMMEND THAT YOUR NORMAL FRIENDS GO OUT AND BUY THEIR OWN COPIES.

fig a: TOO CLOSE. (NOT NORMAL AT ALL!)

IF YOU ARE LISTENING TO NORMAL LIFE ON YOUR RADIO, YOU CAN ENHANCE YOUR AURAL PLEASURE BY MAKING USE OF THE BOOK'S CLEVER <u>AUDIO-VISION</u>™ FEATURE. SIMPLY CUT OUT THE CHARACTER PUPPETS, ASSEMBLE THEM, THEN JIGGLE UP AND DOWN AS YOU LISTEN.

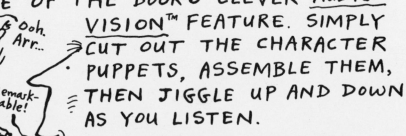

Going down the Bull, Eddie?

Ooh. Arr...

Remark-able!

BUT PLEASE NOTE: THE AUTHOR CANNOT BE HELD RESPONSIBLE FOR DISAPPOINTMENT CAUSED BY LISTENER ERROR, INCORRECT TIME-KEEPING, ETC.

THE CAST OF CHARACTERS

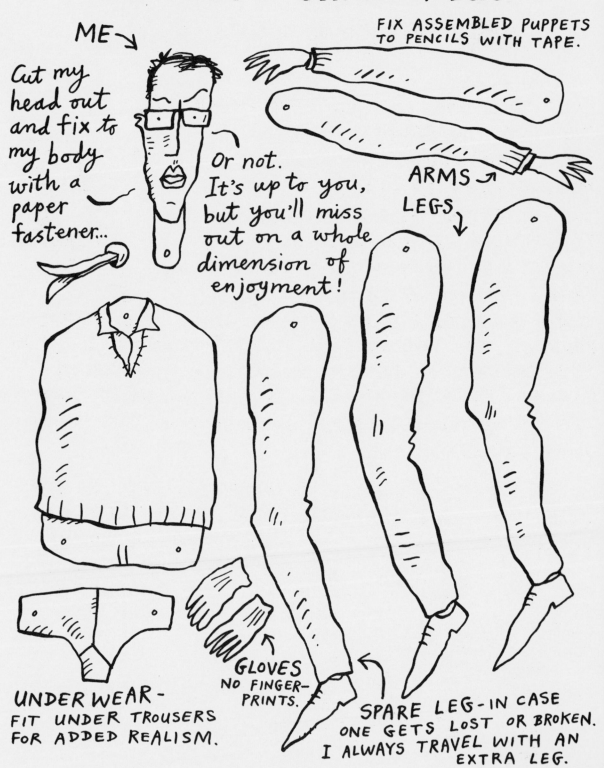

ME →

FIX ASSEMBLED PUPPETS TO PENCILS WITH TAPE.

Cut my head out and fix to my body with a paper fastener...

Or not. It's up to you, but you'll miss out on a whole dimension of enjoyment!

ARMS ↗

LEGS ↓

UNDER WEAR – FIT UNDER TROUSERS FOR ADDED REALISM.

GLOVES NO FINGER-PRINTS.

SPARE LEG – IN CASE ONE GETS LOST OR BROKEN. I ALWAYS TRAVEL WITH AN EXTRA LEG.

ASSORTED MINOR CHARACTERS

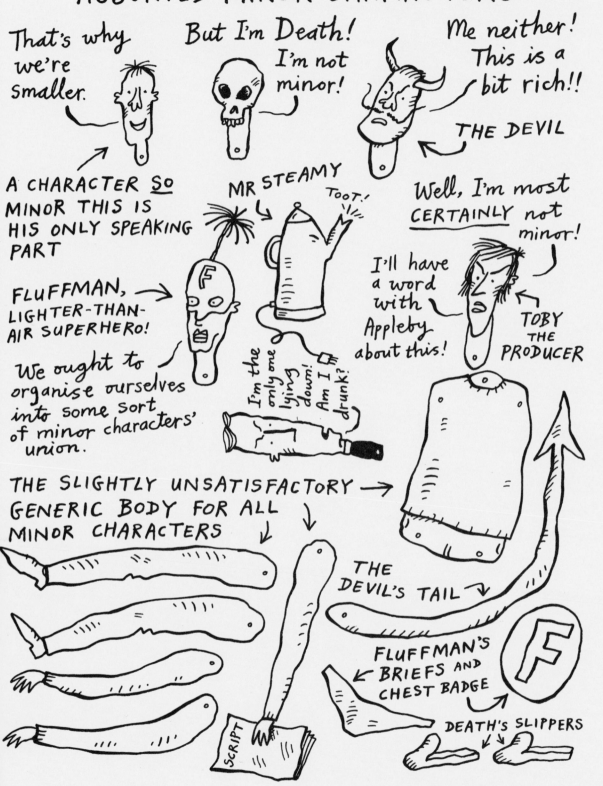

That's why we're smaller.

A CHARACTER SO MINOR THIS IS HIS ONLY SPEAKING PART

But I'm Death! I'm not minor!

Me neither! This is a bit rich!!

THE DEVIL

MR STEAMY

TOOT!

FLUFFMAN, LIGHTER-THAN-AIR SUPERHERO!

We ought to organise ourselves into some sort of minor characters' union.

Well, I'm most CERTAINLY not minor!

I'll have a word with Appleby about this!

TOBY THE PRODUCER

I'm the only one lying down! Am I drunk?

THE SLIGHTLY UNSATISFACTORY GENERIC BODY FOR ALL MINOR CHARACTERS

THE DEVIL'S TAIL

SCRIPT

FLUFFMAN'S BRIEFS AND CHEST BADGE

DEATH'S SLIPPERS

17

Part One
NORMAL LOVE

LET ME TELL YOU ABOUT A FEW OF MY
TRAGIC LOVE AFFAIRS...

MY FIRST SEXUAL EXPERIENCE WAS PLATONIC LOVE, OR FALLING IN LOVE WITH A PLATE.

SIGH!

Hello, darling. Let's, um... you know...

NEXT WAS SELFISH LOVE.

Falling in love with yourself?

No. Falling in love with a shellfish.

SOON I SUCCUMBED TO NOSY LOVE.

I love being nosy.

And I love your nose.

THEN I BECAME OBSESSED WITH A VOLVO...

So sturdy and reliable.

PAT PAT

WHO I ABANDONED FOR A SAAB.

So sporty!

OF COURSE, MR STEAMY SPURNED MY ADVANCES.

Ouch! I only wanted to make a pot noodle!

HISS!

SO I REBOUNDED INTO A TORRID AFFAIR WITH MISS SAUCY.

So squeezy!

Giggle!

CHOC SAUCE

FINALLY, I MET ROGER, JOHN AND SUSAN.

AND WE ALL LIVED HAPPILY EVER AFTER AROUND MY KITCHEN TABLE.

Ho ho ho! We always have a laugh, eh, guys!

20

ANOTHER TRAGIC LOVE STORY...
FLUFFMAN to the RESCUE!

Panel 1: FLUFFMAN, LIGHTER-THAN-AIR SUPERHERO, IS IN LOVE. NOW, READ ON...

GUST...

Panel 2: Oh, Fluffman!

Oh, Miss Maroon!

Panel 3: I LOVE the way you hold me so TIGHTLY, Fluffman!

I have to, Miss Maroon, or I would blow away.

GUST!

Panel 4: Oh, Fluffman! I bet you could pick me up in one hand with your super-strength and carry me over the threshold of your secret fortress.

I guess I could, miss maroon.

Panel 5: Show me your muscles, Fluffy... May I call you Fluffy?

Of course. I'll do a pose for you, Miss Maroon.

Panel 6: Call me Lauren, Fluffy!

Er, Lauren... What a pretty name.

Panel 7: Here we go!

Ooh, you look VERY gorgeous posing in your bikini bottoms, Fluffy!

Panel 8: Ahem. Actually, these are special steel-reinforced crypto-lycra superhero pants, Lauren... Oops! Breeze is picking up...

Panel 9: WAAAAAAA!!

GUST...

FLUFFY!! COME BACK! Don't LEAVE me! You're just like all the others!!

A BRIEF DIGRESSION CONCERNING
The LAND of HEARTS

Is that where hearts live, darling?

That's right, darling.

When two hearts fall in love, two little humans pop into existence above their heads.

And that's how you and I were created, darling!

How romantic!

Isn't it nice to think that every human being came into existence because a heart fell in love!

But does a human being die each time a heart's heart is broken?

POP!

HERE IS THE RATHER WONDERFUL
CUPID COMPASS

mr Depp?

Roger Depp, yes.

JUST PUNCH IN THE REQUIRED CO-ORDINATES, SUCH AS: "HUNKY, WILL WASH THE DISHES, SEXUAL GOD, DREAMBOAT, ETC," THEN LET THE ARROW ON THE COMPASS DO THE REST!

BEEP BEEP

USING AN IMAGINARY CUPID COMPASS, JOURNEY AROUND THE MAP BELOW AND FIND THE IDEAL PARTNER WAITING FOR YOU!

USE THE CO-ORDINATES OPPOSITE ⟶

FROM START MOVE: DOWN 2, LEFT 3, UP 1, LEFT 3, DOWN 5, RIGHT 2, DOWN 4, RIGHT 3, DOWN 2, UP 6, RIGHT 2, UP 1, UP 1, LEFT 7, DOWN 7, RIGHT 1, UP 3, RIGHT 7, UP 1, LEFT 8, UP 1, RIGHT 6, STOP!

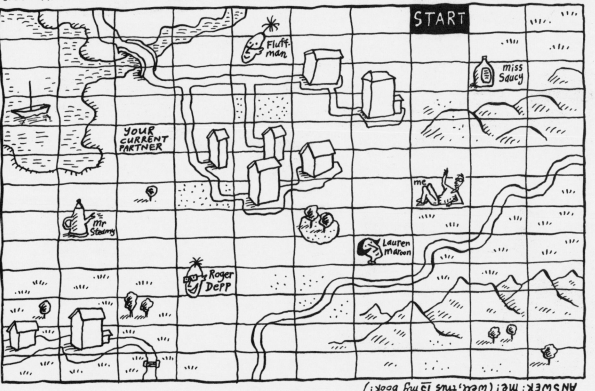

ANSWER: me! (well, this is my book!)

23

Come on, everyone! We're leaving!
Get in! NO! Come back here! I'll count
to three and anyone not in by then
will be... Er, well, I'll think of
something! One! Two! Two and a
half! Two and three-quarters...
Oh, for goodness sake, PLEASE get in!
I'm starting to get cross...

Part Two
NORMAL KIDS

WHEN I WAS A LITTLE KID I HAD AN ALIEN FRIEND...

HIS SPACESHIP HAD CRASHED IN OUR GARDEN AND LAY BURIED UNDERNEATH THE LAWN. AT NIGHT, WEARING HIS SPACE PYJAMAS, HE WOULD FLOAT UP TO MY BEDROOM WINDOW AND WE WOULD SNEAK OUT TO PLAY.

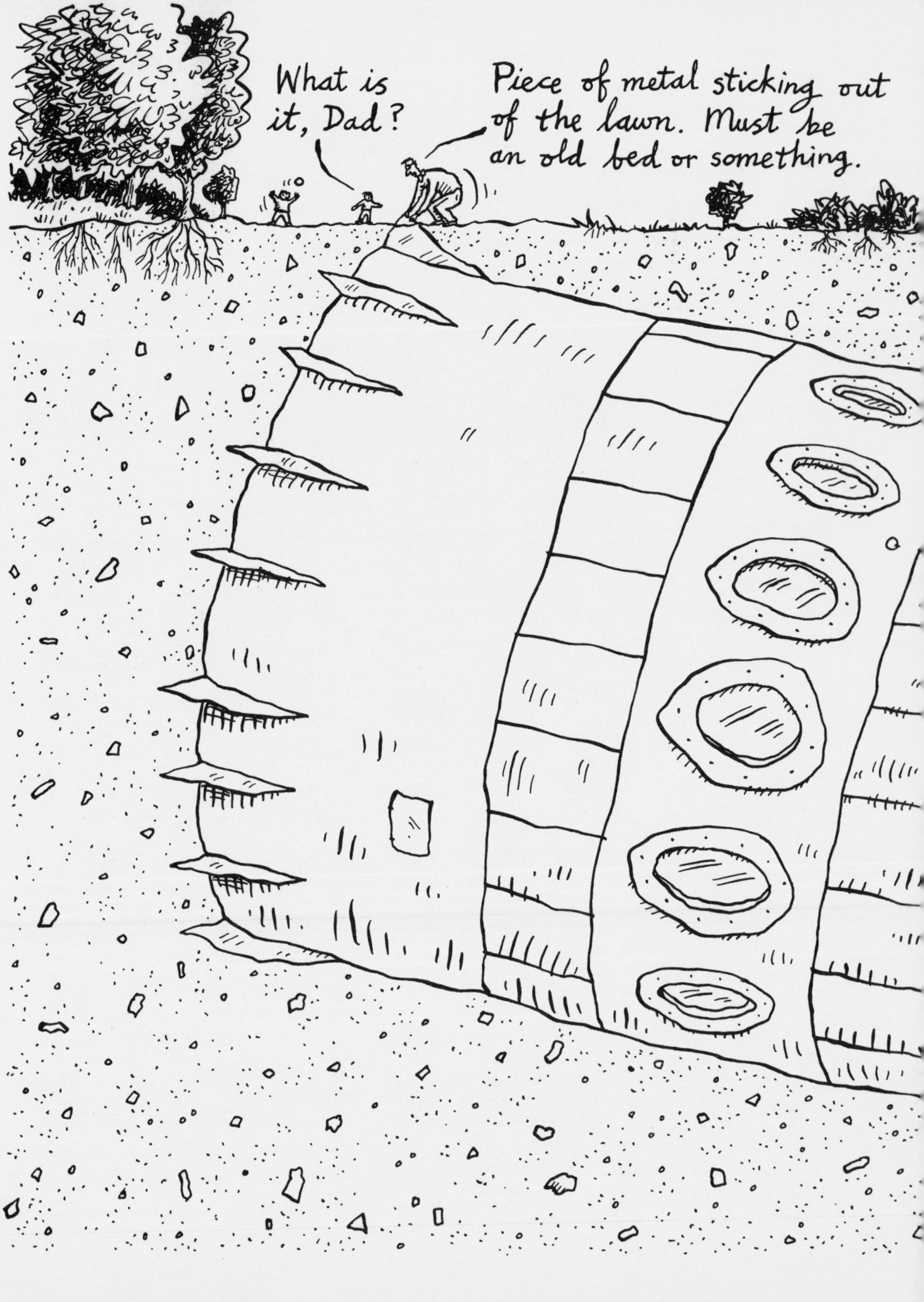
What is it, Dad?
Piece of metal sticking out of the lawn. Must be an old bed or something.

HAVE **YOU** GOT CHILDREN?

IF YOU ARE UNSURE, CONSULT THIS HANDY CHECKLIST OF TELL-TALE SIGNS TO LOOK OUT FOR

1 - NOISE!

I can't hear myself think!

2 - SWEET WRAPPERS & YOGHURT POTS IN FRONT OF THE TV.

3 - THE TELEVISION LEFT ON 24 HOURS A DAY...

Let's go to the hop!

...AT FULL VOLUME!

4 - YOUR BED HAS BEEN JUMPED ON & TRASHED.

5 - THERE ARE DRAWINGS ON THE WALLS.

I did'nt draw this dad

6 - THE TOILET PAPER IS ALL OVER THE BATHROOM FLOOR.

7 - TOY DINOSAURS TURN UP IN UNEXPECTED PLACES.

Ow!

SOCK

STEGOSAURUS

8 - HUGE BAGS OF CHICKEN NUGGETS & OVEN CHIPS IN THE FREEZER.

Where has my vodka gone?

CHECKLIST:

ONLY _ONE OR TWO_ OF THESE SIGNS MEAN MICE, OR SLOVENLY HOUSE-KEEPING.

THREE PLUS - YOU'V GOT KIDS. SET TRAPS.

THE THINGS I USED TO DO BEFORE HAVING KIDS:

1 - NOTHING AT ALL.

BLANK STUPOR

COFFEE GOING COLD →

2 - LIE IN BED ALL DAY READING THE PAPERS.

Hmm. Sausages are being re-designed.

FREE!

3 - STAY UP ALL NIGHT WATCHING FILMS ON TV.

This film is awful!

4 - SUDDENLY, ON THE SPUR OF THE MOMENT, DECIDE TO GO AND VISIT FRIENDS IN CALIFORNIA.

Hi there!

Hey! It's too hot here!

5 - BE HOUSEPROUD.

A cat hair!

Must get rid of that cat!

HOW I FILLED THE HOURS, DAYS AND MONTHS I SHALL NEVER KNOW! IT WAS A SAD AND LONELY LIFE.

THE THINGS I DO NOW THAT I HAVE KIDS:

1 – WEAR SPECIAL, MUD-COLOURED PROTECTIVE WIPE-CLEAN CLOTHING.

SPLOTCH!

2 – WIPE YOGHURT, JAM, JELLY, ETC, OFF OTHER THINGS.

Yuk!

3 – SAY...

No sweets, until you've eaten your nuggets!

Aw...

4 – BE FIERCE!

I SAID NO SWEETS!!

Ha ha ha ha! Look at Dad!!

5 – DEVELOP FACIAL TICS, GREY HAIR AND BAGS UNDER THE EYES.

Ha ha ha ha ha ha! Just look at him now!

6 – WORK MYSELF INTO AN EARLY GRAVE.

Childhood is the happiest time of your life... But it's wasted on kids.

WHEN I WAS A TEENAGER I REMEMBER WORKING HARD.

Wow! Crown Court sure shows life as it really is!

Execute him...

AND AS AN ART STUDENT I WAS DEDICATED TO THE PURSUIT OF KNOWLEDGE.

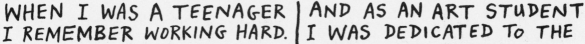

I sentence you to DEATH for shoplifting...

Crown Court is still as thrilling as ever.

NOW THAT I'M A GROWN-UP, I'M STARTING TO NOTICE THINGS ABOUT TODAY'S KIDS WITH ALARM...

Their eating habits just aren't natural!

WE WANT NUGGETS!

For every meal?!

WANT NUGGETS!

THEY USE STRANGE WORDS WHICH MAKE NO SENSE.

It's like an ALIEN LANGUAGE!

Rad tick!

Bola!

You're bologuns!

And it isn't HUMANLY POSSIBLE to do homework, watch TV, surf the Internet, listen to CDs AND talk on the phone ALL AT ONCE!!

I CAME TO THE INEVITABLE CONCLUSION...

Perhaps modern children really AREN'T human!

STAR TREK etc. etc.

ONE DAY I WAS READING THE PAPER AND CAME ACROSS AN INTERESTING ADVERT:

SUSPICIOUS? NEED PROOF? The SHRIVELLED HAND can help! Send us your snippets of information and we'll check it, test it, analyse it and generally take it seriously, however absurd. Fill in ad

WELL, I IMMEDIATELY SENT THE SHRIVELLED HAND SOME NUGGETS FOR ANALYSIS, WITH A COVER LETTER OUTLINING MY OBSERVATIONS.

Can't do any harm...

A FEW DAYS LATER I WAS CLEANING UP CAT VOMIT...

Ugh!

On the kitchen table, too. And it's furry...

...WHEN THE DOORBELL RANG.

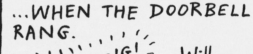

DING DONG!

HOMEWORK

Will one of you kids please answer the door?

DING DONG! DING DONG!

PLEASE get the door, someone! I'm cleaning up cat vomit!

Huh! You ASK and ASK until you're BLUE in the face, then you have to go and do it yourself!!

35

AN EXTRACT FROM:

THE TOP SECRET CULINARY CODES of the SHRIVELLED HAND!

Mmm! That smells good...

I'm afraid it means "I'm having an affair."

ABOUT THE SHRIVELLED HAND:

The Shrivelled Hand exists to help humanity fight for its freedom against the alien hordes who are trying to take over the Earth for what ghastly purposes we can only futilely speculate and hopelessly battle and...

CONTINUED INSIDE

A CHICKEN IN A PARTY HAT

MEANS: "Meet me on the 6·15 train to London tonight."

BREAD PUDDING

MEANS: "I'll be in the restaurant car."

A PIECE OF TOAST MEANS:
"The 6·15 is running a few minutes late."

A PIECE OF TOAST & A ROLL OF TAPE:
"Duck! Aliens are shooting at us!"

A BOILED EGG:
"Respond with the correct password or I'll kill you."

SOON I WAS SETTLED IN MY SEAT ON THE 6·15 TRAIN.

SUDDENLY, A MAN SITTING A FEW SEATS DOWN THE AISLE EXPLODED WITHOUT WARNING.

CURIOUSLY, SEVERAL YEARS PREVIOUSLY A MAN SITTING IN THE SAME SEAT HAD EXPLODED THE LAST TIME I WAS ON THE 6·15.

THEN A WOMAN SCREAMED. LOOKING ROUND, I SAW THAT IT WAS THE SAME WOMAN WHO HAD SCREAMED ON THE OTHER OCCASION.

APART FROM THAT, THE JOURNEY WAS UNEVENTFUL AND SOON I STARTED TO DOZE.

BOOM!

I don't suppose this has anything to do with the plot.

WHEEZE... ZZZZZZZZ SNORT!! Snuffle... GRUNT! ZZZZ

SUDDENLY, I WAS AWOKEN BY A FIRM HAND ON MY SHOULDER.

Dinner is being served in the restaurant car, sir.

WAH! Uh, er... Thank you.

IN THE DINING CAR I QUICKLY READ MY DINNER PLATE.

Hmm. Potatoes, sausage, jelly, a haggis and some chewing gum...

Let's see, that means "Eat nothing, the food is drugged." Gosh!

THEN I HEARD A VOICE.

Psst! Behind you!

?

Who are you?

Grimwaldibus Two, the current head, plural, of the Shrivelled Hand. I have another man living inside me.

Hello from me, too.

Nice to meet you. Both.

But why aren't you eating?

For the same reason as you. All the food on Earth is full of alien brain-controlling drugs!

Good grief!

We are being manipulated by extra-terrestrials!

Just as I suspected! But, why?!

MUNCH CHEW SWALLOW

38

Have you noticed how, in the years since WE were kids, children have become much more boisterous, disruptive and hyperactive?

STEVEN APPLEBY AS A CHILD:

SILENCE

QUIETLY READING A BOOK ABOUT PIRATES.

MODERN CHILD:

SCREAM!

WANT fizzy drinks!

WANT sweets!

WANT new toys!

WANT a pirate costume!

JUMP!

STEVEN'S BEDROOM:

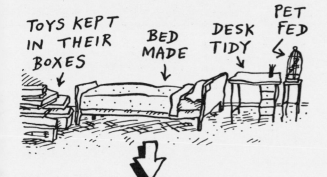

TOYS KEPT IN THEIR BOXES

BED MADE

DESK TIDY

PET FED

MODERN CHILD'S TRASHED BEDROOM:

SWEET WRAPPERS

EMPTY CEREAL BOWLS

ROTTING FOOD

ROTTING PET

HOW STEVEN BEHAVED AT MEAL TIMES:

May I have seconds, please, mama? And a glass of water? Please...

CLEAN PLATE

MODERN CHILD AT MEAL TIMES:

Give me SWEETS!

Don't like CHIPS!

Want FIZZY DRINK!

WANT IT NOW!!

I see what you mean... But what's the reason?

Our real kids have been replaced by uncouth aliens on package holidays!

Gosh! So what are you going to do?

Correction. What are YOU going to do.

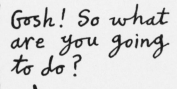

I, personally, was careful not to eat any of the drugged food, but despite my precautions the man living inside me scoffed an entire plate of bread when I wasn't looking.

Sorry... BELCH!

So far I have... resisted the urge to... forget everything I know... about this ghastly plot... and return home. But I... can't fight... the drugs much... longer!

SECONDS LATER MR TWO'S MIND WAS RE-FORMATTED.

Hi ho. Time I was off. Little Josh has his first show-and-tell school assembly tomorrow, then I take Heidi to be fitted for her new brace....

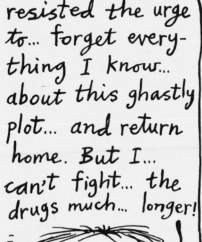

Goodbye... And remember! ONLY EAT FOOD YOU HAVE PREPARED YOURSELF!

I WAS LEFT ALONE ON THE 6·15. METHODICALLY, I SETTLED DOWN TO PREPARE A SIMPLE SUPPER. I GREW WHEAT, HARVESTED IT, GROUND FLOUR AND BAKED MYSELF A LOAF OF BREAD. THEN I MILKED A COW, CHURNED THE CREAM INTO BUTTER AND MADE THE WHEY INTO CHEESE.
IT WAS A BASIC BUT SATISFYING MEAL. I ATE HUNGRILY THEN, EXHAUSTED, FELL INTO A DEEP SLEEP.

...clackety clack clackety clack clackety clack...

NEXT MORNING I AWOKE FEELING REFRESHED AND READY TO SAVE THE WORLD.

Morning, sir. Here's the post.

Thank you.

THE POST WAS A FRUIT FLAN.

It's just a circular asking me to invest my pension in dried frogs.

I THREW THE FLAN INTO THE DUSTBIN.

AS I WAS PUTTING THE CODE BOOK AWAY IN MY BAG I SPOTTED MY WIFE'S SANDWICHES.

Yum!

I WAS HUNGRY AND WITHOUT A MOMENT'S THOUGHT, TUCKED IN.

41

IMMEDIATELY THE WORLD STARTED SPINNING AND I
BEGAN TUMBLING OVER AND OVER, LIGHTS
FLASHING, UNTIL I REMEMBER NOTHING MORE...

43

Part Three
THE NORMAL MIND

SOME OF THE THINKING
PARTS OF THE BODY:

Contrary to accepted scientific
theory, I believe that much
of the MIND is located
OUTSIDE the brain.
To demonstrate this,
I am now completely
naked...

THE NIPPLES —
TWIN SEATS OF
LOGICAL THOUGHT.

THE BELLY BUTTON —
JUDGE OF SPACIAL
AWARENESS.

THE ELBOW — A
WITTY BODY PART

THE PENIS — MEN GET
INTO TROUBLE BY
PLACING UNREASONABLE
INTELLECTUAL DEMANDS
UPON THIS ORGAN.

THE OVERLY IMAGINATIVE
BUTTOCKS — WE TALK OUT
OF THESE WHEN
DISCUSSING A TOPIC WE
KNOW NOTHING ABOUT,
SUCH AS OURSELVES.

& OF COURSE, EVERYONE IS FAMILIAR WITH THE
MENTAL CAPABILITIES OF THE HEART (LOVE),
LIVER (ENVY), SPLEEN (VINDICTIVE ANGER), THUMB
(FOR KEEPING OTHERS UNDER) & BLADDER (DESPERATION).

I RECENTLY HAD MY BRAIN MAPPED, SO HERE'S A TOUR THROUGH THE HIGHWAYS AND BYWAYS OF MY NORMAL MIND...

51

THE ROLLING HILLS OF **SEXUAL OBSESSION**

FOREST of
FEAR OF
DEATH
CONTINUED

THIS PART
OF THE MIND
IS **NOT** DRAW
TO SCALE.
IT IS THE
SECTION
DEVOTED TO
**PENIS-
SIZE
ANXIETY**
AND SHOUL
LAST FOR
SIX PAGES.

THE BOG OF
EMPATHY

Help!

Oh
dear.

Dearie
me. How
sad.

THE ONLY REAL SURPRISE REVEALED
BY THE MAPPING WAS THIS SMALL
AREA:

THIS BRAIN BELONGS TO GEORGE MOULE

MY BRAIN TURNED OUT **NOT** TO BE
MINE AFTER ALL!
I IMMEDIATELY CONFRONTED
MY PARENTS...

Yes, dear. We always meant to tell you...

We MADE you.

Of course you did. You're my parents.

No, son. We actually MADE you. From a kit.

And we bought your brain from a grave robber.

Well! I'm FURIOUS!!

WHY?!

You gave me such a SMALL PENIS!!

It didn't seem important. WE still love you, dear.

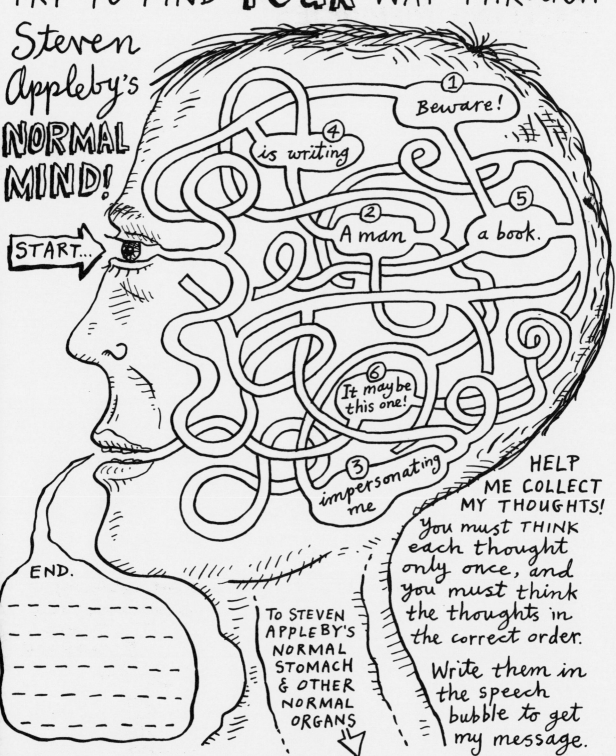

AND NOW... HERE ARE A FEW OF MY MOST EXCITING MEMORIES!

Unfortunately, my memory doesn't seem to work very well.

Another Part
NORMAL FOOD

PHEW! THIS PAGE HAS SOME RELEVANCE AFTER ALL! I THOUGHT MY MIND WAS PLAYING TRICKS ON ME FOR A MOMENT...

Part Four
NORMAL SCIENCE

Some other MIRACLES of MODERN SCIENCE!

FEEDING THE FIVE THOUSAND.

No big deal using these high-energy protein sachets, ketchup-flavoured and shaped like fish.

Astronauts love them.

OINK! OINK!

CURING A LEPER.

Easy. I just shoot him full of antibiotics...

Oops. I'll try the other arm.

SNAP!

DISCOVERING HOW THE UNIVERSE WAS CREATED.

Only one more sub-atomic particle to find and we're there.

Then we can recreate the creation in the lab. Simple.

DISCOVERING HOW TO DESTROY THE WORLD.

Easy peasy.

We can do it blindfolded and with one hand tied behind our backs.

A ROBOT STEVEN APPLEBY.

BURP...

Well, it may be a miracle, but it's not wearing any clothes!

Tut tut...

SHORTLY...

There. He's decent now.

Much better!

A PEEK INTO MY LABORATORY

I'M NOT JUST A CARTOONIST, YOU KNOW. DOWN UNDER THE STAIRS I HAVE A FULLY EQUIPPED LAB!

60

AND HERE IS A SELECTION OF MY
GREATEST INVENTIONS

THE TIME REFRIGERATOR:

It keeps food fresh forever by stopping time!

A CAR WHICH CAN THINK:

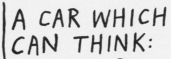

What's the point of life? I feel so depressed...

THE CONNOISSEUR'S TOILET PAPER:

SOFT ON ONE SIDE FOR BUM COMFORT →

HARD ON THE OTHER TO STOP FINGERS GOING THROUGH.

THE PERPETUAL MOTION ROUNDABOUT:

Can I get off? PLEASE? It's been fifteen years...

Wait until it stops.

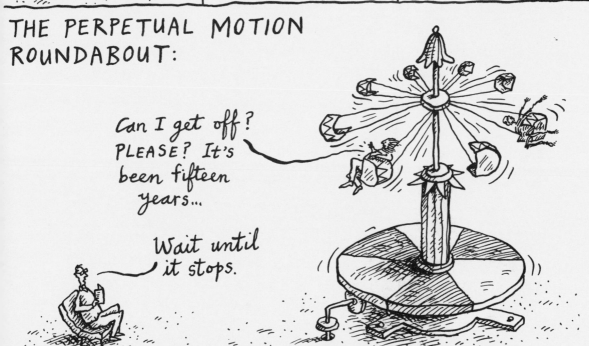

I AM PARTICULARLY PROUD OF CLOUD TRAVEL:

What ON EARTH is "cloud travel"?

Well, as I'm sure you know, humans are 98% water.

This huge steamer converts a person into water droplets or, in other words, a cloud.

Try it.

Okay.

WHOOMPH!!

The cloud "you" then blows across the sky until you reach your destination...

Feels lovely!

... Where you fall to earth as rain.

Whee!

How marvellous! And can you go exactly where you intend?

Er, no. Cloud travel is still a LITTLE imprecise.

Also, when you are back on solid ground you'll find that you've lost 2% of your weight.

?

From the 98% water part?

No. The other 2%.

What do you mean?

I'm afraid all that's left of you is the water.

I've still got a few bugs to iron out.

Now, my new cat-powered telephone, on the other hand...

I don't want to hear about it!

Part Five
NORMAL WORK

Some FATHERLY ADVICE from Steven Appleby's DAD:

The thing is, Dad, I want to ENJOY my work.

Oh dear, Steven! I'm afraid that's NOT the right attitude AT ALL!

Work is intended to fill the time between childhood and old age. It's not meant to be ENJOYED!

What a strange notion, dear.

Hand on heart, I can sincerely say that I didn't enjoy MY work for a single second.

You get to ENJOY yourself at weekends and after you retire.

But I LIKE being a cartoonist, Dad.

If you like it, then it isn't work.

Go and get a PROPER job!

A LOOK AT SOME OF THE PROPER JOBS WHICH KEEP OUR WORLD FUNCTIONING!

THIS YOUNG LADY'S JOB IS TO BURY BONES, FRAGMENTS OF CHINA, EVEN ENTIRE TOWNS!

So that archaeologists will have something to dig up.

HERE'S A LAD ON A JOB-CREATION SCHEME. HE HAS TO CREEP INTO HOUSES AT NIGHT AND MIX UP CDs AND VIDEOS.

I put them in the wrong boxes!

THERE'S AN ENTIRE WORKFORCE EMPLOYED TO STEAL CARS, PICK POCKETS, COMMIT BURGLARIES AND SO ON.

Purely to give the Police Force something to do!

Nee naw nee naw...

AND OVER HERE ARE SOME OF THE TEAM WHO DISMANTLE THE WORLD WHEN YOU GO ROUND A CORNER AND CAN NO LONGER SEE IT.

Gangway!

We'll put this lot next to Alaska.

THESE SCIENTISTS ARE EMPLOYED TO CHANGE THE PHYSICAL LAWS OF THE UNIVERSE FROM TIME TO TIME.

Otherwise research scientists would finish their research and have nothing to do but sit twiddling their thumbs.

I also release new animals and insects just to keep biologists busy.

HERE'S A DOCTOR WHO INVENTS NEW DISEASES AND A MAN WHO BURNS OUT LIGHTBULBS.

Here's one you catch from cereal packets!

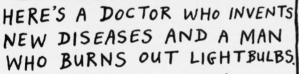

Brilliant!

CLICK
CLICK
CLICK
CLICK
CLICK
CLICK
CLICK
CLICK
CLICK
PHUT!

AND HERE ARE THE VERY IMPORTANT PEOPLE INDEED WHO PULL THE VAST CURTAINS TO ALLOW DAWN TO APPEAR.

Steven Appleby's GUIDE TO CHANGING YOUR CAREER! COME ON! IT'S EASY!

BORED? FED UP WITH THE OFFICE? SIMPLY CLOSE YOUR EYES, MUTTER "ANYTHING WOULD BE AN IMPROVEMENT!" AND PLUNK YOUR FINGER DOWN ON THE PAGE. DON'T CHEAT! HAND IN YOUR RESIGNATION TOMORROW!

Publisher	Washing-machine repairer	Sex therapist	Balloonist	Playwright	Builder
Priest	Animal trainer	Exorcist	Musician	Fisherman or Fisherwoman	Nudist
Coffee-granule checker	Postman	Boss	Analyst of life	Actor/manager	Frog herd
Starer	Sandal designer	Spoon carver	Writer	Hotelier	Plumber
Candlestick maker	Thief...	Speculator	Violin balancer	Shop assistant	Pagan
Surgeon	Soldier	Sailor	Begger-man or woman	Cartoonist	Astronaut
Sturgeon	Lawyer	Stripper	Policeman	Politician	Start your own business
Pilot	Writer	Tea maker	TV presenter	Frogman	Nothing
Chair tester	Chair sexer	Gym instructor	Potato peeler	Doctor	Cook
Cab driver	CD mixer-upper	Page-number checker	Train-track repairer	Artist	Sports personality

WINNER: You! (There are no losers, except G. Moule, if you are reading this).

The TRUTH about WORK!

THE FIRST DAY:

Well, well, well. I've completed my Life's Work in just a couple of hours! Time to retire and put my feet up, I think...

Let me take a look.

I thought so. You've missed a bit there...

Hmm. I see what you mean.

Looks like you're going to be busy for another forty years.

DRAT!

There's nothing like a brisk
walk before breakfast.
The sun is shining, the
birds are singing...
What a GLORIOUS day
to be alive!

Part Six
NORMAL DEATH

LIFE IS, OF COURSE, JUST ONE BRIEF, BLEARY-EYED MOMENT OF WAKEFULNESS IN THE NEVER-ENDING SLEEP OF DEATH.

A small, flickering night-light, burning briefly on Death's dark and draughty bedside table.

BUT DEATH MAY AWAIT YOU, DEAR READER, BUT IT IS NOT FOR ME!

INSIDE...

Morning, Mum! Morning, Dad!

Morning, Steven, old lad. I see the Minister in charge of bicycle-seat springing has resigned.

Morning, honey! my, you're looking younger every day!

HERE'S A CONTRACT FOR YOU TO FILL IN FOR YOURSELF, READER:

CONTRACT

REF _ _ _ _ _ _ _
DOC _ _ _ _ _ _ _
N/CD _ _ _ _ _ _ _
(ADMIN ONLY)

THIS CONTRACT IS BETWEEN _ _ _ _ _ _ _

↳ YOUR NAME & ADDRESS ↲

_ _ _ _ _ _ _ _ _ _ _ _ _ _ OF _ _ _ _ _ _ _

_ _ _ _ _ _ _ _ _ _ _ _ _ _ _ _ _ _

& SATAN (ALSO KNOWN AS BEELZEBUB, THE DEVIL, ETC.) OF THE VILLAS, HOT SPRINGS, MELTING FLESH, HELL.

I, SATAN, PROMISE TO*_ _ _ _ _ _ _

_ _ _ _ _ _ _ _ _ _

_ _ _ _ _ _ _ _ _ _

_ _ _ _ _ _ _ _ _ _

*INSERT SOME TRIVIAL & SMALL-MINDED LITTLE ITSY-BITSY CHORE (YAWN...) SUCH AS "MAKE ME A MILLIONAIRE" OR "MAKE ME YOUNG AGAIN", ETC.

SMALL PRINT: There's no getting around it. You're still going to die, then you'll go to Hell and suffer for all eternity and more.

IN RETURN FOR WHICH THE ABOVE MENTIONED AGREES TO GIVE ME HIS/ HER SOUL TO DO WITH AS I LIKE. SIGNED:

- Satan ↗ _ _ _

SIGNED (YOUR NAME HERE):

_ _ _ _ _ _ _

PRINT:

_ _ _ _ _ _ _

PLEASE WRITE CLEARLY USING YOUR OWN BLOOD.

74

78

DOCTOR LAUREN MAROON'S SEMINAR ON
WHAT HAPPENS AFTER DEATH...

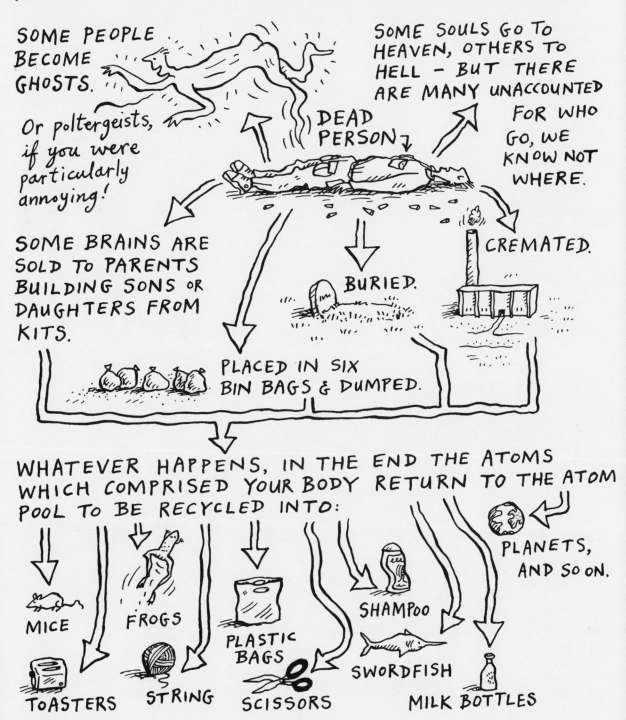

SOME PEOPLE BECOME GHOSTS.

Or poltergeists, if you were particularly annoying!

DEAD PERSON

SOME SOULS GO TO HEAVEN, OTHERS TO HELL – BUT THERE ARE MANY UNACCOUNTED FOR WHO GO, WE KNOW NOT WHERE.

SOME BRAINS ARE SOLD TO PARENTS BUILDING SONS OR DAUGHTERS FROM KITS.

BURIED.

CREMATED.

PLACED IN SIX BIN BAGS & DUMPED.

WHATEVER HAPPENS, IN THE END THE ATOMS WHICH COMPRISED YOUR BODY RETURN TO THE ATOM POOL TO BE RECYCLED INTO:

PLANETS, AND SO ON.

MICE

FROGS

PLASTIC BAGS

SHAMPOO

TOASTERS

STRING

SCISSORS

SWORDFISH

MILK BOTTLES

JUST A FEW OF THE INCONVENIENT PRACTICAL CHANGES CAUSED BY DEATH:

Have you seen Death yourself, Doctor Maroon? In person?

Oh yes. He comes here quite often.

Can you describe him?

Better than that. I know someone who took a photograph of Death only this morning.

The photographer's name is Professor Grimwaldibus Two, and he is also an expert on eternal youth.

Thanks, Doctor Maroon. I'm on my way!

SOON I WAS AT PROFESSOR TWO'S HOUSE.

That must be the Professor hiding behind that statue of Peter Pan As A Very Old Man.

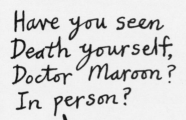

Professor... Good God! You're ANCIENT!! I was told you are an expert on eternal youth!

Well, I'm not!

That's right. HE'S not an expert, but I am!

Who said that?

The other man who lives inside me said it...

...Because I'm the expert!

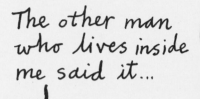

Why do you look so old if you know the secret of eternal youth?

The man inside me knows the secret...

And I keep it for myself...

...You little runt!

...Because I discovered it, not you!

Gentlemen, I hear that you also have a photograph of Death. May I see it?

Certainly...

I LOOKED AT THE PHOTOGRAPH FOR A LONG TIME. IT WAS OF NICE, OLD MR HIVES, OUR NEXT-DOOR NEIGHBOUR!

Incredible!

This explains why he was going to Great Aunt Fiona's!

I'm going to confront Mr Hives and find out when I am due to die!

84

WELCOME!
& THANK YOU FOR CHOOSING THE KINGDOM of HEAVEN!

JUST LOOK at these INCREDIBLE facilities!

GOLF ... UNIQUE 79-HOLE COURSE!

PING-PONG 8000 TABLES!

SKIING NEW WARM SNOW!

BOUNCING UP AND DOWN!

POT-HOLING SHALLOW HOLES!

2 NEW POOLS OPENING THIS YEAR!

DON'T WORRY IF YOU CAN'T SWIM — THERE'S NO FEAR OF DROWNING BECAUSE YOU'RE ALREADY DEAD!

On the beaches...
BENEFIT FROM YOUR OWN DECK CHAIR, LOTS OF BEACH CAFÉS & OVER 70 ICE-CREAM VANS!

TOWELS ARE PROVIDED FREE OF CHARGE, BUT YOU MUST BRING YOUR OWN TRUNKS.

6 GREAT RESTAURANTS!
10 BARS &
47 DISCOTHÈQUES!

Benny's PIZZA!

ALL UK NEWSPAPERS ARE AVAILABLE — A COUPLE OF DAYS LATE, LIKE ON THE CONTINENT. SATELLITE TV IS FITTED IN EVERY ROOM. SHEETS ARE 100% COTTON. EACH PERSON GETS TWO PILLOWS.

MOBILE PHONES ARE ALLOWED, BUT PLEASE USE THEM WITH DISCRETION SO AS NOT TO ANNOY OTHER RESIDENTS.

It looks MARVELLOUS! Blue skies, sand, sea, sun and fluffy white clouds. But what about food? Are vegetarians allowed into Heaven?

God forbid, sir! And He certainly does! Vegetarians are, indeed, FORBIDDEN to enter the Kingdom!

All God's creatures, however, __DO__ go...

So you'll find that all the familiar cuts and joints of meat are available in abundance.

Mouth-watering!

Where do I sign?

Right here.

Hmm. That's unusual. You've got red ink in your fountain pen.

INK?

That's not ink. It's BLOOD. I used it to sign a contract with Beelzebub.

86

90

No resemblance to anyone
in my real family,
living or dead, including
myself, is intended.

OTHER BOOKS by Steven Appleby,
which you might, or might not, enjoy:

NORMAL SEX

MEN - THE TRUTH

MISERABLE FAMILIES

THE SECRET THOUGHTS OF
MEN, WOMEN, BABIES, CATS,
DOGS & YOURSELF

ANTMEN CARRY AWAY MY THOUGHTS
AS SOON AS I THINK THEM

ALIEN INVASION - THE COMPLETE
GUIDE TO HAVING CHILDREN

THE TRUTH ABOUT LOVE

ENCYCLOPEDIA OF
PERSONAL PROBLEMS

STEVEN APPLEBY is a member of the
NUDE RADIO BROADCASTERS of GREAT BRITAIN

WWW. steven appleby .com